PIANO • VOCAL • GUITAR

S0-CCN-826

51 COUNTRY STANDARDS

HAL•LEONARD
CORPORATION
7777 W. BLUEMOUND RD. P.O. BOX 13819
MILWAUKEE, WISCONSIN 53213

ALL I HAVE TO DO IS DREAM

By BOUDLEAUX BRYANT

(Hey, Won't You Play)
ANOTHER SOMEBODY DONE SOMEBODY WRONG SONG

Words and Music by LARRY BUTLER
and CHIPS MOMAN

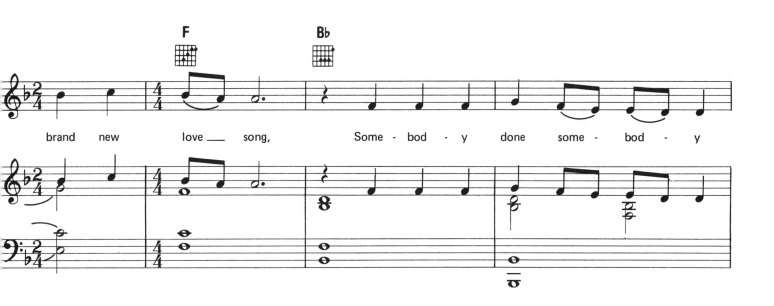

ANY DAY NOW

Words and Music by BOB HILLIARD
and BURT F. BACHARACH

BLUE SUEDE SHOES

Words and Music by CARL LEE PERKINS

Bright Tempo (not too fast)

Chorus

Well, it's one for the mon-ey, two for the show,

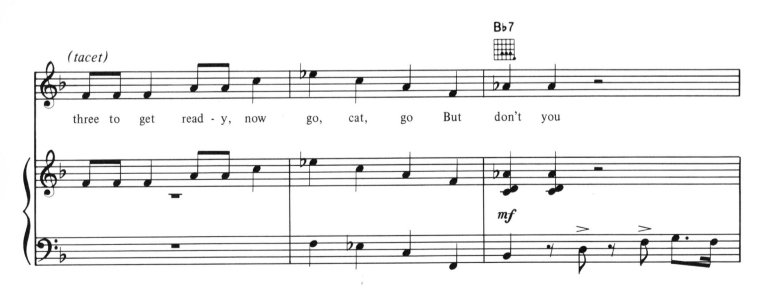

three to get read-y, now go, cat, go But don't you

ANY TIME

Words and Music by
HERBERT HAPPY LAWSON

ARE YOU LONESOME TONIGHT?

Words and Music by ROY TURK
and LOU HANDMAN

BY THE TIME I GET TO PHOENIX

Words and Music by
JIMMY WEBB

CAN'T STOP MY HEART FROM LOVIN' YOU

Words and Music by JAMIE O'HARA
and KIERAN KANE

COLD, COLD HEART

Words and Music by
HANK WILLIAMS

COULD I HAVE THIS DANCE

Words and Music by
WAYLAND HOLYFIELD and BOB HOUSE

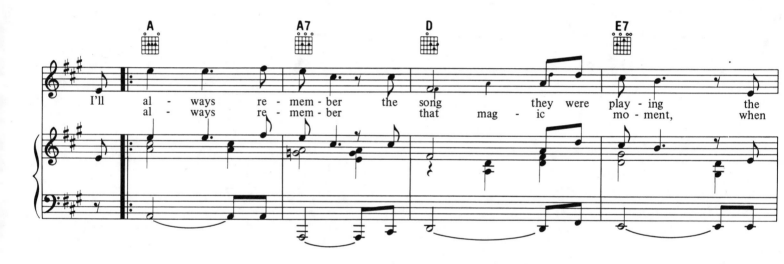

I'll al - ways re - mem - ber the song they were play - ing, the
al - ways re - mem - ber that mag - ic mo - ment, the when

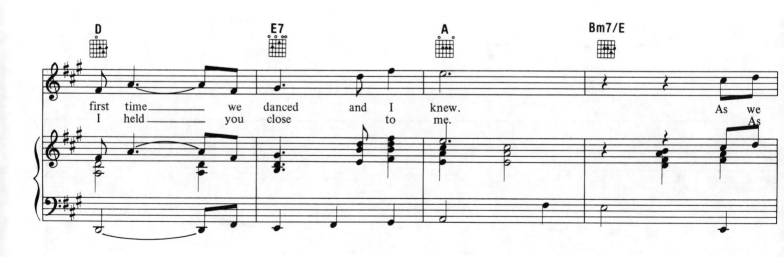

first time_____ we danced and I knew.
I held_____ you close to me.

As we
As

COUNTRY SUNSHINE

Words and Music by DOTTIE WEST,
BILL DAVIS and DIANNE WHILES

CRAZY

Words and Music by WILLIE NELSON

DADDY SANG BASS

Words and Music by
CARL PERKINS

Moderately fast

I re- mem-ber when I was a lad, times were hard and things were bad; But there's a

sil- ver lin- ing be- hind ev-'ry cloud._ Just poor peo-ple that's all we

DADDY'S HANDS

Words and Music by
HOLLY DUNN

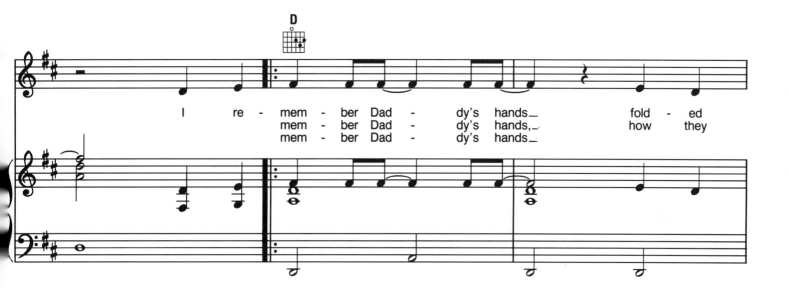

I re - mem - ber Dad - dy's hands____ fold - ed
mem - ber Dad - dy's hands,___ how they
mem - ber Dad - dy's hands____

si - lent - ly in prayer,____ and reach - ing out to hold____
held my Ma - ma tight____ and pat - ted my____ back
work - ing 'til they bled,____ sac - ri - ficed____ un - self -

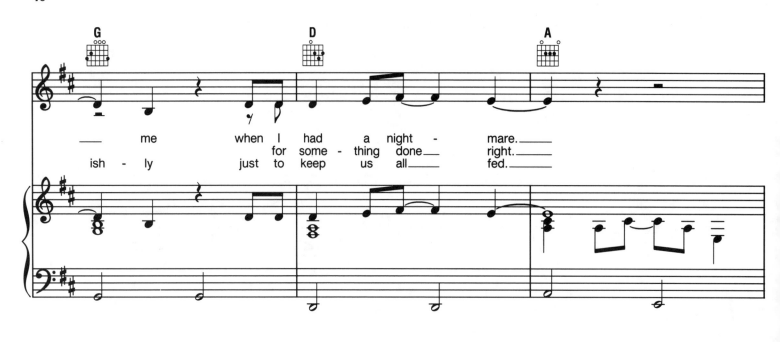

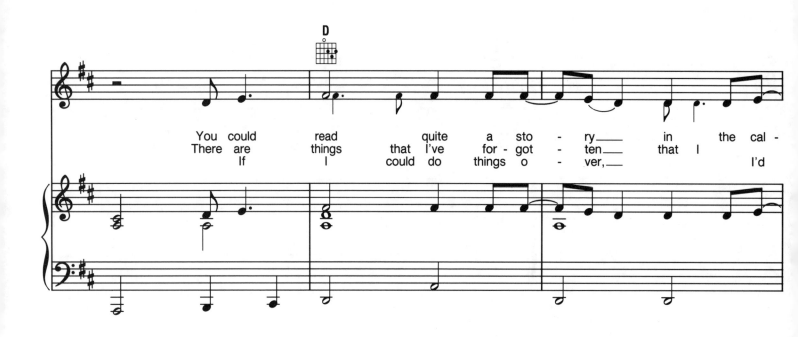

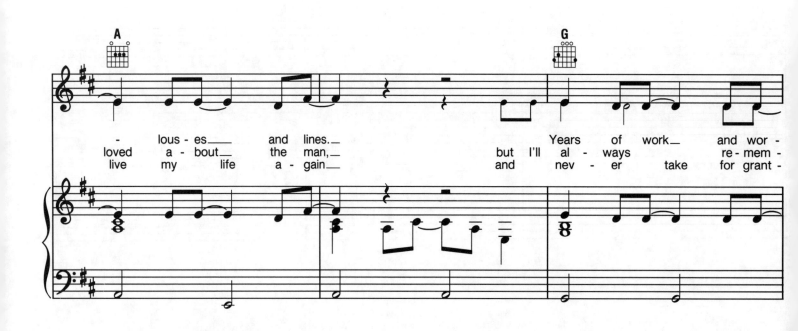

42

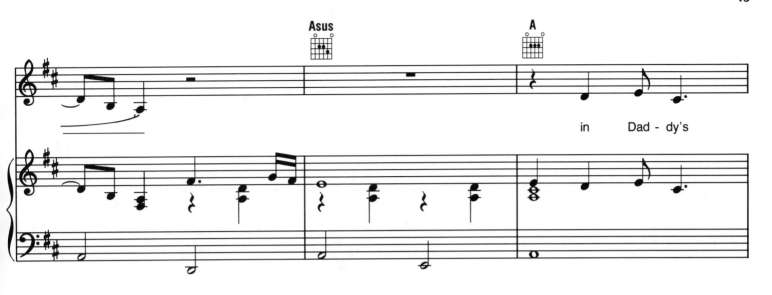

in Dad - dy's

hands.

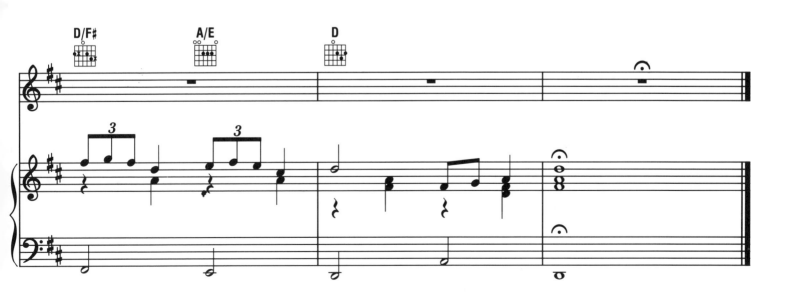

DETROIT CITY

Words and Music by DANNY DILL
and MEL TILLIS

Hard-Driving rhythm

EL PASO

Words and Music by MARTY ROBBINS

Moderato

Out in the West Tex - as town of El Pa - so, I fell in
Night - time would West find me in Ro - sa's can - ti - na, Mu - sic would

love with a Mex - i - can girl. _____
play and Fe - li - na would whirl. _____

47

FOREVER AND EVER, AMEN

Words and Music by DON SCHLITZ
and PAUL OVERSTREET

MCA MUSIC PUBLISHING

52

53

GOD BLESS THE U.S.A.

Words and Music by
LEE GREENWOOD

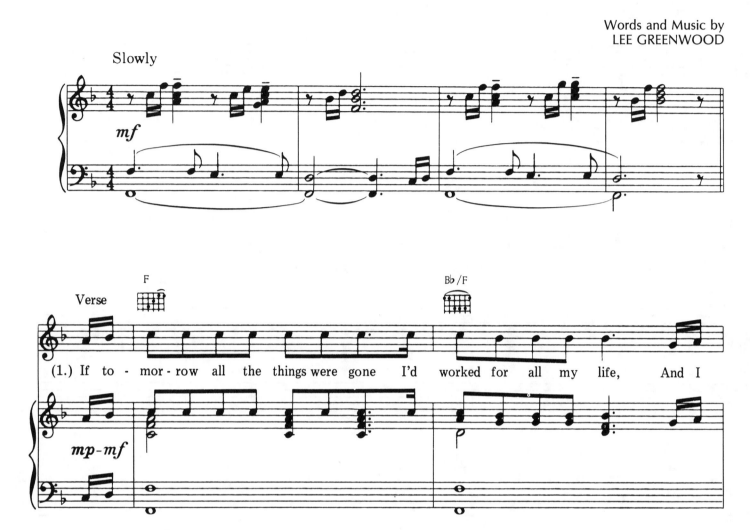

MCA MUSIC PUBLISHING

60

GREAT BALLS OF FIRE

Words and Music by OTIS BLACKWELL
and JACK HAMMER

GRANDPA
(TELL ME 'BOUT THE GOOD OLD DAYS)

Medium Slow Country

Words and Music by
JAMIE O'HARA

(sung 8va lower)

Grand - pa,   tell me 'bout the good old days._
Grand - pa,   ev - 'ry - thing is chang - in' fast. _

Some - times _____ it feels _____ like   this world's gone cra -
We call _____ it prog - ress,   but I just don't know. _

GREEN GREEN GRASS OF HOME

Words and Music by CURLY PUTMAN

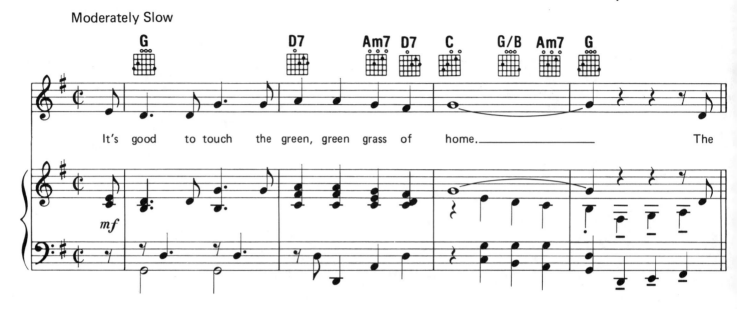

I DON'T CARE IF THE SUN DON'T SHINE

Words and Music by MACK DAVID

HE STOPPED LOVING HER TODAY

Words and Music by
BOBBY BRADDOCK & CURLY PUTMAN

Verse 3:

He kept some letters by his bed, dated 1962.
He had underlined in red every single, "I love you".

Verse 4:

I went to see him just today, oh, but I didn't see no tears;
All dressed up to go away, first time I'd seen him smile in years.
(To Chorus:)

Verse 5: *(Spoken)*

You know, she came to see him one last time.
We all wondered if she would.
And it came running through my mind,
This time he's over her for good. (To Chorus:)

HEARTACHES BY THE NUMBER

Words and Music by
HARLAN HOWARD

CHORUS

Now I've got heart-aches by the num-ber, trou-bles by the score. Ev'-ry day you love me less, each day I love you more. Yes, I've got heart-aches by the num-ber,___ a love that I can't win, but the day that I stop count-ing, that's the day my world will end._____ day my world will end._____

HEARTBREAK HOTEL

By MAE BOREN AXTON,
TOMMY DURDEN and ELVIS PRESLEY

I FALL TO PIECES

Words and Music by HANK COCHRAN
and HARLAN HOWARD

Moderate Country 2

I
fall _____ to piec - es _____ each time I
fall _____ to piec - es _____ each time some-

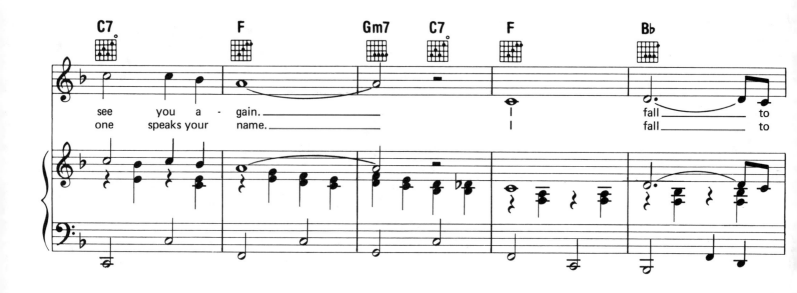

see you a - gain. _____ I
one speaks your name. _____ I fall _____ to
fall _____ to

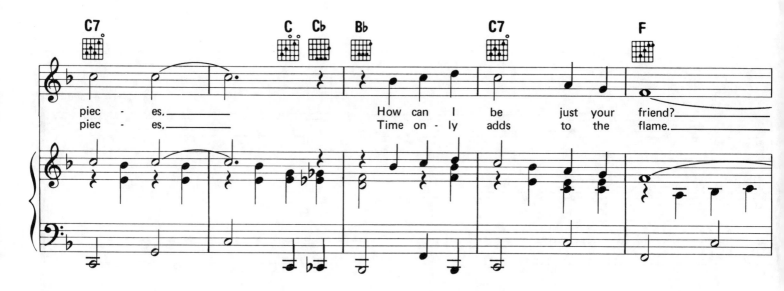

piec - es. _____ How can I be just your friend? _____
piec - es. _____ Time on - ly adds to the flame. _____

I SAW THE LIGHT

Words and Music by
HANK WILLIAMS

85

ISLANDS IN THE STREAM

Moderately Slow Rock

Words and Music by BARRY GIBB,
MAURICE GIBB and ROBIN GIBB

Ba - by when I met you there was peace un - known.
I can't live with - out you if the love was gone.

I set out to get you with a fine tooth comb. I was soft in - side___ there
ev - 'ry - thing is noth - ing if you got no - one and you___ did walk in the night___ slow-

___ was some - thing go - in on.___ thing.___
- ly lo - sin sight of the real thing.___ But

90

IT'S NOW OR NEVER

Words and Music by AARON SCHROEDER
and WALLY GOLD

JAMBALAYA
(ON THE BAYOU)

Moderately

Words and Music by HANK WILLIAMS

3. Settle down far from town, get me a pirogue
   And I'll catch all the fish in the bayou
   Swap my mon to buy Yvonne what whe need-o
   Son of a gun, we'll have big fun on the bayou

LITTLE GREEN APPLES

Words and Music by
BOBBY RUSSELL

KING OF THE ROAD

Moderately, with a bounce (♩♩ = ♩³♪)

Words and Music by ROGER MILLER

LUCILLE

Words and Music by ROGER BOWLING
and HAL BYNUM

MAKE THE WORLD GO AWAY

By HANK COCHRAN

MAMMAS DON'T LET YOUR BABIES GROW UP TO BE COWBOYS

Country Waltz

Words and Music by ED BRUCE
and PATSY BRUCE

MY ELUSIVE DREAMS

Words and Music by CURLY PUTMAN
and BILLY SHERRILL

1. You fol-lowed me ____ to Tex-as, You fol-lowed me ___ to U-tah,
2, 3 *(See additional lyrics)*

We did-n't find it there so we moved on. ___ You

fol-lowed me ____ to Al-a-bam', Things looked good in Bir-ming-ham,

2. You had my child in Memphis, I heard of work in Nashville,
We didn't find it there so we moved on.
To a small farm in Nebraska to a gold mine in Alaska,
We didn't find it there so we moved on. (Chorus)

3. And now we've left Alaska because there was no gold mine,
But this time only two of us move on.
Now all we have is each other and a little memory to cling to,
And still you won't let me go on alone. (Chorus)

ON THE OTHER HAND

Words and Music by DON SCHLITZ
and PAUL OVERSTREET

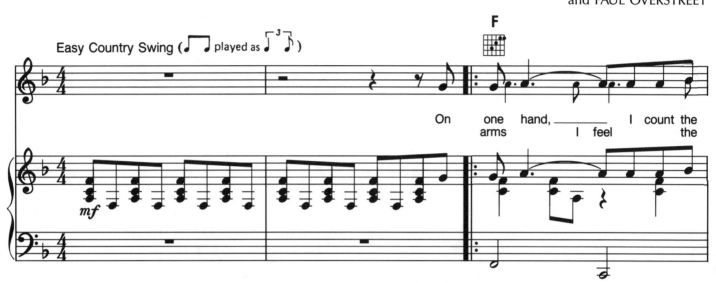

MCA MUSIC PUBLISHING

117

ROCKY TOP

Words and Music by
BOUDLEAUX BRYANT and
FELICE BRYANT

Lively

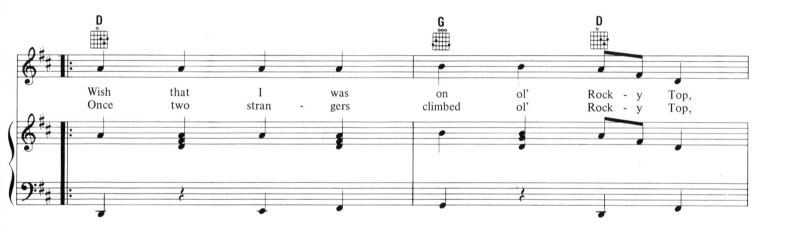

Wish that I was on ol' Rock-y Top,
Once that two stran-gers climbed ol' Rock-y Top,

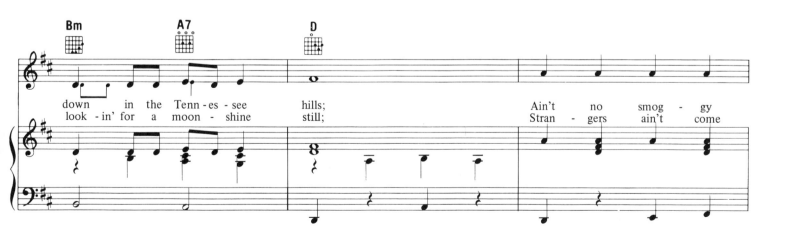

down in the Tenn-es-see hills; Ain't no smog-gy
look-in' for a moon-shine still; Stran-gers ain't come

Chorus

Rock - y Top, you'll al - ways be home sweet home to

me; Good ol' Rock - y Top;

Rock - y Top, Tenn - es - see; Rock - y Top, Tenn - es -

see; see. see.

D.S. al 3rd
Ending

Verse 3:
I've had years of cramped-up city life
Trapped like a duck in a pen;
All I know is it's a pity life
Can't be simple again. (Chorus)

RUBY, DON'T TAKE YOUR LOVE
TO TOWN

Words and Music
By MEL TILLIS

SATIN SHEETS

Moderately Slow

Words and Music by
JOHN E. VOLINKATY

can't hold me tight___ like he does___ on a long, long night.___

You know___ you did - n't keep me sat - is -

fied.___

fied.

D.S. al Fine

2. We've been through thick and thin together,
   Braved the fair and stormy weather
   We've had all the hard times, you and I.
   And now that I'm a big success,
   You called today and you confessed
   And told me things that made me want to die.

3. You told me there's another woman
   Who can give more than I can,
   And I've given ev'rything that cash will buy.
   You can't buy me a peaceful night,
   With loving arms around me tight
   And you're too busy to notice the hurt in my eyes.

STAND BY ME

Words and Music by BEN E. KING,
JERRY LEIBER and MIKE STOLLER

Slowly

When the night_____ has come and the land is dark   And the moon_____ is the on - ly_____ light we'll see,   No, I won't be a - fraid, no_____ I_____

SIXTEEN TONS

Words and Music by MERLE TRAVIS

SMOKY MOUNTAIN RAIN

Words and Music by KYE FLEMING
and DENNIS MORGAN

Easy Swing

I thumbed my way from L. A. back to Knox - ville;
I waved a dies - el down out - side a ca - fe;

I found out those bright lights ain't where I be - long.
He said that he was going as far as Gat - lin - burg.

From a phone booth, in the rain, I called to
I climbed up in the cab, All wet and cold and

THROUGH THE YEARS

Words and Music by
STEVE DORFF and MARTY PANZER

TO ALL THE GIRLS I'VE LOVED BEFORE

Moderately slow, with expression

Words by HAL DAVID
Music by ALBERT HAMMOND

To all the girls I've loved be-fore,
once car-essed,
shared my life,

who trav-eled in and
and may I say I've
who now are some-one

out my door;
held the best;
els - e's wife;

I'm glad they came a - long,
for help-ing me to grow,
I'm glad they came a - long,

I ded - i - cate this
I owe a lot, I
I ded - i - cate this

142

TULSA TIME

Words and Music by DANNY FLOWERS

WALKING THE FLOOR OVER YOU

Words and Music by
ERNEST TUBB

Swingy tempo

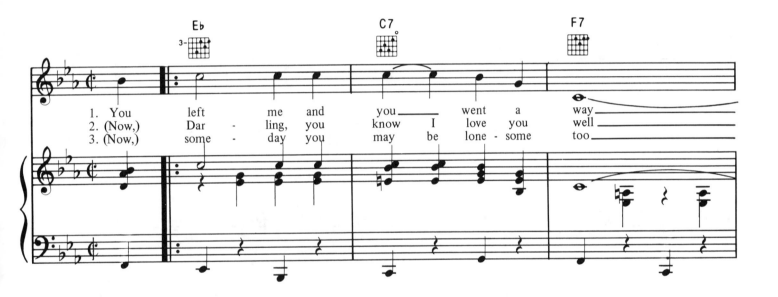

1. You left me and you____ went a way____
2. (Now,) Dar - ling, you know I love you well____
3. (Now,) some - day you may be lone - some too____

You said that you'd be back in just a day____
Love you more than I can ev - er tell____
Walk - ing the floor is good for you____

WATERLOO

Words and Music by JOHN LOUDERMILK
and MARIJOHN WILKIN

YOU DON'T KNOW ME

Words and Music by
CINDY WALKER and EDDY ARNOLD

YOU NEEDED ME

Words and Music by RANDY GOODRUM

YOUR CHEATIN' HEART

Words and Music by HANK WILLIAMS